BEST WAYS TO INVEST IN PLATINUM AND PALLADIUM

For Beginners

M. L. Pilgrim

KENOSIS BOOKS: INVESTING IN PRECIOUS METALS SERIES

SUBSCRIBE AND GET YOUR FREE eBOOK!

If you are looking for investment that offers you inflationary protection and that reduces your investment risk significantly, precious metals such as gold, silver, and platinum (amongst others) is the way to go. Unlike paper money, precious metals have a finite supply and you cannot print more of them, and because of this, precious metals offer authentic insurance against political and financial upheavals. This book will share about the ff:

WHAT ARE PRECIOUS METALS?
WHY YOU SHOULD INVEST? - THE UPSIDE AND DOWNSIDE
WHO SHOULD INVEST?
WHAT PRECIOUS METALS SHOULD YOU INVEST IN?

WAYS TO INVEST IN PRECIOUS METALS
CONCLUSION- WHEN SHOULD YOU INVEST?

The primary aim of this eBook is to open young investors' eyes to the infinite possibilities of investment in precious metals. This eBook shows you that you have the time advantage of youth and the ability to take on more risks, and that these advantages can help you make better and bigger investment profits, whether you choose to invest in gold, palladium, copper, silver, or platinum and whether you choose to invest in coins, bars, rounds, or precious metal ETFs.

So take action, and scan the QR CODE and/or Subscribe to our newsletter for more updates!

TO MY WIFE AND MY SON, THIS BOOK IS FOR YOU.

any kind are declared or implied. Readers acknowledge that the author is not engaged in the rendering of legal, financial, medical or professional advice. The content within this book has been derived from various sources. Please consult a licensed professional before attempting any techniques outlined in this book.

By reading this document, the reader agrees that under no circumstances is the author responsible for any losses, direct or indirect, that are incurred as a result of the use of the information contained within this document, including, but not limited to, errors, omissions, or inaccuracies.

Table of Contents

Introduction

Investing is one of the best ways to build wealth in the 21st century, especially because the only traditional way of making money has been to earn it by working a 9 to 5 standard job. Not only is being employed by a business encouraged but it has always been painted as the only way to sustainably make money, and while it is very important to generate a monthly income from having a regular job, there are many more ways to make money today.

When it comes to investing, people shy away from the very topic because they think it's either too complex, too risky, or that they don't have enough money to invest or waste on it, particularly if they don't understand it. The problem with this type of mentality is that instead of doing research and proving or debunking the excuses one has to not invest, many people just drop the topic of investments altogether. Looking at the boom and the crash of cryptocurrencies in 2018, which had many people's hopes up, followed by massive losses and discouragement, it is no doubt that many would think again before investing in cryptocurrencies once more, even if it has recovered.

The unpredictability of taking hard-earned money and investing it into something that you either don't understand or don't trust will always be there. However, you can change your mind about investments, in general, such as taking time to review how well the trade of minerals is performing on the global market and pique interest where it is due.

While it's always necessary to be cautious of where you invest your money, it's also imperative to take risks that are calculated. By monitoring the trading markets, you can invest in minerals like platinum and palladium successfully without taking any losses at all. Instead of just hearing about how other people have managed to hit a jackpot with trading and can enjoy making extra money on the side or saving up for retirement faster, you can achieve the same results. The secret is to go in slow and to not be too hasty about making money with trading, whether it's by investing in minerals or cryptocurrencies. The difference between investing in the two is obviously that investing in minerals is less risky than cryptocurrencies because the algorithm of trading minerals has sense to it, while cryptocurrencies have a mind of their own.

Although there is nothing wrong with working at a job and making the same salary every month, this is still a good thing, you can't exactly build your wealth in this way, not substantially that is. Even if you earn a high-paying salary, you still have the opportunity to increase it significantly and safely too, and that's through investing in minerals. Due to its safety, strength, and stable return rates, you have the potential to earn a lot of money over time. By not investing, you are missing out on a variety of opportunities to increase your financial worth. Even if there is always a risk involved of losing money with any type of investment, by investing wisely, your potential to gain money is much higher than it would be if you didn't invest at all.

Some of the top reasons to invest in platinum and palladium include:

- Growing your money by generating wealth sustainably over time.
- Saving up for retirement faster or increasing the amount you initially thought you would retire with.
- Earning a much higher return than the money you are already making.
- Reaching financial goals quicker, which can aid in fulfilling savings plans or be accumulated to reach certain goals or dreams, like starting a new business.
- Building on pre-tax dollars, which allows you to save more money than what you would have if you only invested post-tax dollars.

Before you continue with the contents of this book, please note that I am not a financial advisor and that the information in this book is purely for educational purposes. Therefore, it is advised that you conduct your own research to support your knowledge on platinum and palladium investments.

Chapter 1: What Are Platinum Group Metals (PGMs)?

While silver and gold are the leading minerals on the precious metal investment market and are usually what people turn to as a safe investment, attention is also shifting to platinum, palladium, and other minerals like rhodium, and for a good reason too.

Platinum Group Metals, or PGMs for short, consist of six elements, including platinum (Pt), palladium (Pd), and rhodium (Rh), which are considered the main metals, but also iridium (Ir), osmium (Os), and ruthenium (Ru), the lesser-known trio of metals. Focusing mainly on platinum and palladium, PGMs in general are recognized as significant additions to an investment portfolio, especially because it offers investors bigger opportunities to diversify existing holdings, along with gaining a full coverage of precious metals. Whether you are a beginner investor or have been in the game for a while, it is important to not put all of your eggs in one basket.

So, while you may have started out investing in gold for wealth preservation or silver for greater price movements that may seem either risky or are more likely to generate profit, and yes, even crypto on the side, investing in PGMs can bring you a lot of value because of their relative stability. PGM investments resemble the trends seen with silver due to both silver and PGMs gaining attention gradually with time. This is one of the biggest reasons why their prices have fluctuated in the past decade.

PGMs are all found in similar mineral deposits, and as a result, share similar chemical properties that are even rarer than gold and silver. The six PGM metals make up 0.0005 ppm of the crust of the Earth, according to the US Geological Survey. They are also located in concentrated geographical locations, and for this reason, mining them requires complex procedures and refining processes. This is also why the prices of these metals are constantly rising.

South Africa is the number one producer of PGMs and holds 88% of global PGM resources. The remaining 12% can be found in Zimbabwe, Russia, Canada, and the US For these reasons, with rarity being one of the biggest, PGMs are far more strongly affected by external economic, labor, and political factors.

Apart from these metals being precious and in high demand as a result, they also serve a significant function outside of investments as they are used as vehicle autocatalysts, are used to make jewelry, and have many chemical, petroleum, glass, electrical, and dental work industrial uses. Since PGMs have complex extraction processes, there are limited concentrations of stockpiles, and political and labor issues also play a role, the supply of PGMs remains constrained. For this reason, they are in high demand, which means that their popularity and profitability is gaining traction incredibly quickly.

Chapter 2: Why Invest in Platinum?

Everyone knows that there is a limited amount of gold on Earth, yet it's still far from being the rarest mineral of all. Platinum, believe it or not, is 30 times rarer than what is considered to be the most mined precious metal in the world, gold. Nevertheless, due to its rarity, next to all of the other PGMs, platinum is considered to be one of the most liquid commodities, which is why it's popular among precious metals brokerages and large retail markets. As with silver, platinum possesses price support from the industrial and jewelry economic sectors.

Like many precious metals, China has the world's biggest platinum jewelry market, which accounts for more than half of the annual demand, while India is the top driver of growth, with demand increasing 10-fold in just 7 years, as a result of a significant rise in the men's jewelry market. Besides being used to fill a jewelry market niche, platinum is often used in systems responsible for controlling electronic goods and vehicle emissions. The precious metal also gets used to create liquid crystal displays and increases hard disk storage density for servers and laptops (Sharps Pixley, n.d.).

Although platinum is also used when building diesel cars, there has been a decrease in demand recently because of emission legislation in many cities. However, potential key drivers for a greater demand in the future could be fuel cell electric vehicles (FCEV).

Roughly 3% of platinum is currently being held for investment purposes as there has been a higher demand for platinum bullion, and it's expected that this demand will increase even more going forward. This is due to investors that are seeking to expand their horizons in the metals sector. Although platinum prices have recently seen a five-year low, platinum has maintained a very strong presence in the precious metal trading market as it has only dropped below the price of gold twice in the past thirty years, making it a very safe investment. Despite recently experiencing a five-year low period in price, platinum is expected to increase in price higher than ever in the future due to its high demand and decreased supply.

Uses of Platinum

As a silver-white metal, platinum was previously known as white gold. It is known to be one of the most resistant types of metals due to its resistance against corrosion and tarnishing, making it a noble metal. It is also very soft and malleable—which means it is easy to shape and stretch into wire—ductile, and unreactive. It doesn't oxidize and is also unaffected by acids. For this reason, there are many uses for it, which is why it's gaining more popularity and is in increasing demand.

Platinum is very closely related to gold, silver, titanium, and copper, and is known as a transition metal among these metals. Transition metals all have an atomic structure that allows them to bond much more easily with a variety of other elements, which is one of the biggest reasons why platinum and other transition metals are commonly used to build parts for motor vehicles and other types of transportation.

Platinum is a very dense element, one of the densest in fact, at 12.4 ounces per cubic inch, according to Chemicool. This means that its density is over 21 times that of water and 6 times the density of a standard diamond. It has an atomic number or number of protons in the nucleus of 78. Its atomic symbol is Pt, and its molecular weight is 195.1. It is solid at room temperature, has a melting point of 3,215.1 degrees Fahrenheit, and a boiling point of 6,917 degrees Fahrenheit. It also has 6 natural isotopes, which are atoms of the element with the same number of protons and a different number of neutrons, and 37 artificial isotopes (Ross, 2016).

In history, the first written record of platinum was in 1557 by Julius Scaliger in Central America. He named the precious metal "Platina", which translates to "little silver". However, it is believed that the metal was used in Egypt and the Americas for jewelry or to make decorative pieces that were mixed with gold. In 1741, Charles Wood, a British scientist, published a study to introduce platinum to the world. He explained in the study about the metal's attributes and potential to be used for commercial applications (Ross, 2016).

In 1748, Antonio de Ulloa, a Spanish scientist published a new description suggesting that the metal was unmeltable and unworkable. However, in the 18th century platinum became known as "white gold". Two British chemists, William Hyde Wollaston and Smithson, were able to produce and sell platinum that was purified using techniques that Wollaston developed. This involved dissolving platinum ore in a nitric and hydrochloric acid mixture. Once the platinum was separated from the remaining solution, the PGMs, including palladium, rhodium, iridium, osmium, and later even ruthenium were discovered in its waste. The technique used to extract platinum and the remaining

PGMs is still being used to this very day, and the byproducts are melted at extreme temperatures to produce the remaining metals (Ross, 2016).

Without this discovery, the six PGMs would have been left undiscovered today. Could you imagine if Wollaston and Smithson had thrown away the waste left behind after discovering platinum? Surely, someone would have discovered it eventually, right? However, if it had taken any longer to be discovered, people wouldn't have been able to put it to good use as they have over the past two centuries. This would have been a game-changer, especially because platinum, along with the other PGMs, served a significant purpose over the years.

For instance, in the past two centuries, a cylindrical hunk of mineral and platinum alloy has been used to measure a kilogram (kg). This has been used globally since the 1800s, and in 1880, 40 of these cylinders, which measure 1 kilogram to 2.2 pounds (lbs.), were distributed as a method of weight measurement worldwide. So, if platinum was never discovered, we would still be trying to figure out how to weigh things in kilograms (Ross, 2016).

Another typical use of platinum is to make jewelry, which has become a very big business in the past few years due to an increase in demand for men's jewelry. Platinum is specifically combined with the five remaining PGMs to create highly durable jewelry, as well as parts of tools and machinery.

In medicine, it is used in many anticancer drugs due to its low reactivity levels, with 50% of all cancer patients that are in therapy using drugs containing platinum, according to Johnstone Park and Lippard Lab in a 2014 study. Among the platinum-containing drugs, cisplatin is also used for cancer and tumor treatment in animals, according to veterinarian Barbara Forney.

Additional medical applications include making dental crowns and pacemakers, along with other equipment that is used for procedures that place material into the human body. For procedures like this, a metal like platinum is needed due to its resistance against corrosion and lack of reactivity in the body and bodily fluids, which make it very safe to use (Ross, 2016).

Advantages

As the rarest of all precious metals, platinum is also considered to be one of the most sacred elements because it is mined in a mere few locations around the world. Today, over 50% of the platinum that gets mined, primarily from South Africa, is used for industrial purposes, particularly to make jewelry. Platinum jewelry is in demand due to its appearance, which has a cool white sheen, its hypo-allergenic properties, and its durability. All of these combine to make it the most expensive metal, which means that whoever buys it can make a significant return on it as an investment over time too (Quality Diamond, n.d.).

Apart from the obvious advantages, platinum is known to accentuate the sparkling effect of diamonds because it doesn't cause the color to reflect in the stone. For this reason, many diamond and jewelry retailers design and manufacture engagement and wedding rings, along with other jewelry pieces that contain diamond or precious stones, with platinum.

Since it is extremely durable, it also serves as an appealing option for long-wear as it is highly stress-resistant and can withstand extreme temperatures, both hot and cold. Although platinum is stress-resistant, it does look better with wear, which means that even if it is placed under stress, it looks better over time. For this reason, men favor platinum as it provides a stylish but rugged look. If it gets any surface scratches, it becomes more appealing, yet the metal can be restored to its original state by a jeweler. This precious metal doesn't contain any nickel, which also means that it is the ideal long-wear metal for allergy sufferers.

Since platinum has become even more in demand over time, there is a clear picture of how well the precious metal will perform in the future. In 2019, platinum managed to outperform both gold and silver, two of the precious metal's biggest competitors. While silver had a 17% spike in 2019, gold led with 20%, but platinum surpassed them both with 24%.

This is the first time in ten years that platinum outshined gold and silver, but not only that, all three precious metals have exceeded their expectations and have spiked in price higher in 2019 than they have since 2009. These returns are very impressive for investors, which is why they have continued to buy even more platinum, gold, and silver in 2020 and beyond.

In 2020, the World Bank predicted that the price of platinum would be $890 per ounce, while the Commerzbank predicted it to be $950 per ounce. However, it turned out that neither of these respected financial institutions was correct. Instead, the price of platinum increased to $1,004 by the 23rd of January 2020. After reviewing this substantial increase in a short period, the World Bank forecast a price increase of 64% for platinum to $1,300 by the year 2030 (Rand, 2020).

From March 2020 until January 2021, the price of platinum has increased by 41% to $1,100. Even with its continuous growth, however, the precious metal is still considered undervalued next to gold and silver (Platinum Investment, 2021).

Disadvantages

Why does platinum remain undervalued?

Well, the popular precious metal largely has its scarcity and exclusivity to blame for it. It is 25 to 30% more expensive to buy platinum than the same amount of gold, which is why many people prefer gold. There are also many disadvantages to mining platinum. One of the biggest reasons why it is more expensive than gold is because it is much more difficult to mine. Nevertheless, many people are interested in platinum and prefer it over gold due to its durability, which is why retailers have taken great interest in it (Brainly, 2018).

Mining, in general, isn't good for the environment because it has a negative impact on the ecosystem. It can cause erosion, deforestation, sinkholes, result in the loss of biodiversity, the potential overuse of water resources, wastewater disposal issues, contamination of soil, surface water, and ground, acid mine drainage, and health issues in miners.

This is the case for mining most types of minerals, yet the cost of mining PGMs, like platinum, raises a unique set of environmental concerns, such as the generation of large volumes of waste rock and tailings, up to 98% of mined material. It also uses lots of electricity, around 175 gigajoules per kilogram mined—that's enough to heat two houses for a year. Platinum mining also releases on average 40 tons of carbon dioxide and uses 400 cubic meters of water per kilogram mined. Although platinum is mined in small quantities due to limited resources worldwide, the natural resources required for the mining of PGMs, in general, have an effect on the environment (Glaister and Mudd, 2010).

Platinum vs. Gold

There are only four minerals that are considered to be precious metals, and these include gold, silver, platinum, and palladium. These are all very valuable metals, which is why they are classified as precious, but they are also elemental metals with a high economic value. Most of these have even been used as a currency, others are valued for their rarity.

Precious metals are also classified as such due to their common corrosion-resistant trait that is used in currency, jewelry, and investments. Among the four metals, gold and silver have always held the spotlight, but now, gold and platinum often get compared as two of the most valued, even though platinum is considered a rare precious metal.

When it comes to appearance, the main distinguishing characteristic of gold versus platinum is its color. While platinum is naturally white, gold is naturally yellow. Both of these precious metals are most commonly used to make engagement and wedding rings, which offer a variety of white and gold options, especially for men. Jewelry retailers often call gold by the term "yellow gold". While some do call platinum "white gold", in the jewelry industry, white gold is not the same thing. White gold rings consist of gold, rhodium, and alloy plating, which makes them look similar to platinum.

Although white gold and yellow gold have the same amount of purity, for example, 14k of either type of gold contains 58.59% gold, the alloys and the presence of rhodium plating in white gold are responsible for making the metal appear white. However, the alloys in yellow gold do not.

Now, since platinum and white gold often get mistaken for each other, one may wonder what the difference between the two is on the jewelry market. For instance, how do people distinguish or find a difference in appearance or value between the two? Well, while white gold is very similar to platinum in appearance, especially at first, platinum is of a higher quality than white gold because, over time, the rhodium plating in white gold wears off. This causes the color to fade and take on a yellowish tinge, which is something that not many people are aware of when they opt for white gold.

Thus, white gold is a cheaper option next to platinum, which does not fade or turn yellow. Although white gold does not last very long, white gold rings can be re-polished and re-plated to look white again (Himmatramka, 2015).

The discoloration of white gold is considered a big problem and often is not made known to people who buy them until it's too late. In the case of buying a product, such as a ring, that is made from white gold, it is in a person's best interest to get a lifetime warranty to re-polish and re-plate the rings they buy.

When it comes to value, platinum rings are heavier and are much purer than gold, yet they are similar in price per ounce for the most part. Since platinum is denser than gold, retailers are likely to use more platinum for one ring than that of rings made from gold, which is why you may find that platinum rings are more expensive than gold rings.

While platinum rings usually consist of 95% pure platinum, a 14k gold ring consists of only 58.5% gold and an 18k gold ring of 75% gold. It is also more expensive to buy platinum versus gold. However, this is only because you're receiving more platinum than you are gold when you purchase a ring made from precious metals.

Platinum versus gold offers greater value for money for this reason, but also because, when gold gets scratched or damaged, some of the gold is removed from the ring or coin and lost. However, if platinum is scratched or dented, the platinum simply moves and is not lost thus maintaining its value (Himmatramka, 2015).

Even if platinum can be scratched and still keep its value, many people don't want this to happen. To achieve this or to restore the quality of platinum, it should be polished regularly. Note that in the case of platinum, polishing will simply move the metal back into place so that the ring becomes smooth. This is distinct from white gold, which will become thin over time.

When it comes to comfort, because platinum is denser than gold, it is heavier. Some people prefer lighter rings or jewelry, while other people prefer the opposite, and this is why both gold and platinum have a strong hold on the jewelry market.

Trading Profitability

One of the biggest questions potential investors have about platinum is, is it an affordable investment compared to gold? When the average individual wants to start investing, especially someone that has not traded before or someone that isn't knowledgeable about trading and financial markets, there is a tendency to gravitate towards investing in gold. While gold is a very good investment and can even be considered one of the best, platinum gives you more value for your money. Platinum is also much more durable than gold, and this combined with its rarity and numerous uses mean it is really in a trader's best interest to seek out platinum as a primary investment.

Has platinum done well for itself consistently over time? No, not per se. But is it one of the best investments you can make, next to other PGMs, now and going forward? Yes, without a doubt. That's because investing in platinum allows you to bet on industrial growth, a weak US Dollar, and a supply or demand imbalance.

When it comes to betting on industrial growth, the auto industry is one of the biggest that make use of platinum to construct products. In fact, one in every five products manufactured in the auto industry uses platinum at some point during its construction. Given that the motor vehicle industry is so big and that cars are constantly in need of parts, whether old or new around the world, platinum will always be in demand.

Although there is a limited amount of platinum in the world, the trend of recycling precious metals is growing. With economies continuing to emerge, there is an increased demand for manufactured goods, which is why a platinum investment is a good bet to make on a global scale compared to other metals or investments.

Platinum investments also act as a hedge when the US dollar weakens, as it is similar to commodities in that its price moves inversely with the US dollar. This makes investing in platinum a way to profit from the negative effects of a weakened dollar. Since the United States is the most powerful nation and biggest economy in the world, it also has a large number of debts and deficits. With this, the US government can print dollars at an unlimited pace to pay its debt, which results in a loss of purchasing power. However, by investing in platinum and similar hard assets, there is protection against the erosion of wealth, which usually occurs because of a weakened US dollar.

Since platinum has a limited supply and is mainly held by a couple of countries, it contains much more value than more popular precious metals like gold and silver. Even though supplies of gold and silver are limited, they are much more abundant than platinum. In response to lower prices, companies have shut down many mines and decreased the production of platinum and other

PGMs. Possible events that can lead to a spike in the prices of PGMs include the following:

- Safety failures at platinum mines.
- Mining strikes, specifically in South Africa.
- Higher global exhaust emission standards.
- Increased consumer demand from developing countries.

Given that the supply of platinum and other PGMs is already constrained, any of these factors can significantly increase platinum prices.

While the first step to knowing whether you should invest in anything, whether it be a precious metal, a company, or even Bitcoin, starts with understanding what you are investing in, the next question you should ask yourself is: Should I invest in Platinum?

Good question, right? Looking at the pros versus the cons of investing in platinum, whether you are a beginner trader or not, will tell you that you should. Even if you start small, investing in platinum can earn you good returns. However, apart from the obvious reason why people invest, platinum is also a very good addition to your portfolio, specifically for diversification purposes. If you want an impressive investment portfolio, you don't have to only look at stocks, commodities, and bonds to play it safe, you can also invest in PGMs. With platinum, investors can also make a profit from growth in the industrial and automotive industry, which over time, can continue to benefit investment portfolios.

Trading platinum offers plenty of advantages, especially for growing economies that continue to expand because the citizens of those countries are likely to consume more manufactured goods. By investing in platinum, investors can capitalize on this trend without needing to invest in any local emerging country's stock markets. By investing in platinum, an investor can profit from a weak dollar as well as from consumer spending, offering a steady investment that always continues to grow.

Potential factors to take note of that can make trading with platinum risky include the development of automotive emissions-reducing technology, a slowed down auto sector or a global recession that may depress prices, and the federal government tightening or a continually strengthened US dollar. Nevertheless, platinum is an affordable and safe investment option, according to John LaForge, the head of Asset Strategy at Wells Fargo. There are long-term fundamentals that include an increase in using platinum all around the world, including for constrained supplies and in industrial applications (Pines, 2021).

Buying Platinum Jewelry as an Investment

Gold is still considered one of the best investments you can make when it comes to buying jewelry. However, so is platinum. While gold used to be thought of as the most luxurious statement piece you could wear, platinum, among other metals, has now taken over and gained all the hype.

As a white metal, and known as the Metal of Kings, platinum is favored for its rarity. This is why many people would rather opt for a platinum ring, watch, or other pieces of jewelry over gold these days. This doesn't mean that gold has lost its value whatsoever. It simply took a step back to make space for one of the leading PGMs.

When buying platinum jewelry, just like trading metals on the markets, you are investing in it. Even though platinum has only gained a lot of attention recently, it has been around forever. In fact, it began to be used in jewelry 200 years ago. Prior to its use in jewelry, the metal was discovered by Spanish Conquistadors during the 1600s. At the time, platinum was thought to be misunderstood as an unusable sub-form of gold. It took jewelers till the 1800s to figure out that platinum could also be molded into jewelry, of which the first was made in the French King Louis XVI's court, where it became associated with royalty. King Louis XVI also declared it as the only metal fit for Kings, which is why it is recognized as such.

Platinum, otherwise known as the King of Metals, is valuable for more reasons than one. Apart from being 30 times rarer than gold, 10 tons of platinum ore must be mined to produce 1 oz of pure platinum. Needless to say, mining enough to create platinum jewelry or use it for anything else takes a lot of work, which is just another reason why it is so expensive.

Another reason why it is so valuable is that it does not fade as white gold does. Platinum is also the purest metal to make jewelry from.

Gold is 24k in its purest form and cannot hold its shape for long. For this reason, gold gets mixed with other metals, like copper and nickel, to make jewelry. As a result, the gold jewelry that a person buys in-store typically has 58% or 75% gold purity. 22k is the highest purity of gold, followed by 18k, and then 14k. In contrast, platinum is a very hard metal, so it doesn't need to be mixed with other metals to maintain the jewelry's shape. While platinum jewelry is not 100% pure, it contains 95% platinum, which adds to its value even more.

Another benefit of platinum is that it is hypoallergenic. This means that anyone can wear it, and it is especially well-suited to those with sensitive skin. This is another significant reason why many prefer platinum jewelry. Since it is extremely durable and strong, jewelers often favor it above gold, as they know people are willing to pay for quality engagement rings and wedding bands.

To identify platinum, you can do the following:

- **Look for the platinum hallmark** - This mark will be written as Pt or PLAT on the ring and may be followed by numbers like 950 or 999 to indicate purity. This written mark is the best way to get quality assurance.
- **Test the metal with the scratch test** - This is a test that distinguishes between platinum and silver. Since platinum is a very hard metal, the test involves running your nail along platinum jewelry's surface. Should the metal scratch, it's either silver or platinum that contains a lot of silver. If it doesn't scratch, it means that you have a very pure form of platinum.
- **Test the metal with the magnet test** - Platinum, among other precious metals is non-magnetic. To determine if your PGM metal is real, you can place a magnet close to it. Should the jewelry react, it's not platinum, although it could be platinum alloy.

Buying platinum jewelry is quite simple. All you must do is buy a piece of platinum jewelry, just be sure to test that you're buying platinum jewelry with a high purity. The more platinum jewelry you own today, the more money you are likely to resell it for in the future, even in as little as a year from now.

Platinum Mining Stocks

To invest in platinum mining companies, you'll need to purchase shares of those companies on the stock exchange. The top five platinum mining companies as well as the total amount of platinum they own are shown below:

1. Anglo American Platinum - 2.05 million ounces
2. Impala Platinum Holdings - 1.31 million ounces
3. Sibanye Stillwater - 1.08 million ounces
4. Northam Platinum - 900,000 ounces
5. Norilsk Nickel - 700,000 ounces

By investing in one or multiple of these leading platinum mining companies, whether you have a small or large number of shares, you can decrease the risk of being negatively affected by downturns in the spot price of platinum.

Another option is to invest in ETFs that are backed by platinum. This can allow you to include exposure to platinum mining companies and other companies that deal with platinum all with one purchase. You can also invest in the platinum futures market or as mentioned, purchase shares in platinum mining companies. Platinum or precious metals indexes also exist to guide the choices that you make with your investments. Should you have a way to store it, you can also buy platinum the same way you would buy gold and silver.

Many of the same companies that operate in the business of platinum also mine palladium, and the top five listed above are also the top five palladium mining stocks to invest in. These companies work to explore, develop, and mine precious metals to process and purify them according to their customers' requirements. The mining companies are responsible for finishing products such as dental, jewelry, and decorative items. All of the above-mentioned platinum and palladium stock mining companies also belong to the broader precious metals sector within the stock market index.

Mining stocks can be measured in value by using a stock screener that includes a variety of different platinum mining stocks. The results show that mining stocks perform on par with other popular stock investments such as Next-Gen stocks, energy stocks, technology, healthcare stocks, advertising or media, textiles or apparel, computer or IT, etc.

Aberdeen Standard Physical Platinum Shares ETF

As products responsible for providing exposure to an industry in a single purchase, ETFs are underlying holdings that can include platinum and other companies, all of which deal or trade with platinum. Platinum ETFs include the benefits that ETFs offer, including diversified holdings and tax benefits in comparison to mutual funds. Like ETFs covering other sectors, platinum ETFs can also be leveraged.

The Aberdeen Standard Physical Platinum Share ETF (PPLT) is one of the top platinum ETFs and is issued by Aberdeen Standard Platinum ETF Trust. The investment objective of the Trust is for the shares to reflect the performance of platinum's price. The shares and investments made by the ETF were designed for investors that want a cost-effective way to invest in platinum.

Aberdeen Standard Physical Platinum Share ETF can be traded on trading platforms online. As of June 2021, PPLT was trading at $109.34. While there are short-term price fluctuations, as is common for ETFs and stock shares, a strong upward trend has continued over the past year, indicating the profitability of platinum ETFs.

Chapter 3: Why Invest in Palladium?

While platinum is among the more commonly heard of precious metals next to gold and silver, palladium also fulfills a very crucial role, particularly in the global manufacturing industry. One of the most common uses of palladium occurs in the automotive industry and accounts for 85% of all palladium use worldwide. The palladium is used in a car part called the catalytic converter, which catches hydrocarbons and other pollutants and converts them to environmentally safe emissions. It is also used to build electronics, to conduct electricity, to make jewelry, in old photography printing equipment, coins, and water treatment equipment (Sharps Pixley, n.d.).

Like platinum, palladium is also among the rarest, but most in-demand precious metals. It was first isolated by

William Hyde Wollaston in 1803, the same man who discovered rhodium within a short period after. Palladium is 15 times rarer than platinum, which makes it even more valuable, yet it only gained popularity during the Second World War. In the 1940s, the government outlawed the platinum trade which caused palladium to grow in stature (Sharps Pixley, n.d.).

Palladium is relatively new among precious metals, so you may have never heard about it before because it has yet to gain widespread popularity among investors. Even so, due to its rarity, it is a very valuable and safe investment. It's also quite appealing due to its accessible price point.

With significant surges resulting from labor laws and political factors in South Africa where it is mainly mined. Indeed, these market forces caused the price of palladium to quadruple in a 1.5-year timespan following 2010. Although there were some marked downturns in the following years, the price recovered in 2017 as it steadily climbed from less than $700 per ounce to $1,050 in just 9 months (Sharps Pixley, n.d.). After 2017, the price continued to climb, and in April 2021, it reached $2,648, which displays just how valuable palladium is and how fast it is increasing in value over time (Monex, n.d.).

Like with platinum, palladium's value is one of the main reasons why investors buy it. When you are a beginner investor, an investment in any precious metal, especially

PGMs, can take you a long way and gain respect among other investors.

The great thing about palladium is that even though it's considered one of the most precious and undervalued metals, not everybody is aware of it. When you do research on what to invest in, you probably won't see PGMs in the mix. That's because they are fairly new to the market. Palladium is an often-forgotten metal, which is something you can take advantage of. Palladium investing is still in its early stages and its value will continue to increase over time.

Since there will always be a need for this precious metal, there is no doubt that demand for it will persist over time. With strong growth in the past few years, palladium has continued to display gains of over 1,000% since 2008. While investors mainly focus on gold and silver, palladium is a good metal to invest in if you like to turn away from the crowd. One thing is for sure, it's definitely a conversation starter and can get you far portfolio-wise.

Uses of Palladium

In 2021, palladium is trading higher than gold, and even though this is the case, both gold and palladium are doing exceptionally well. One of the biggest factors that have placed a spotlight on palladium include, just like with platinum, is the auto industry, which has resulted in strong demand for palladium. The auto industry accounts for three-quarters of the world's demand for palladium, especially because it is primarily used in the manufacturing of catalytic converters. For this reason and the demand for vehicles in major markets like China and the US, the bearing on palladium's price has continued to increase.

Apart from the auto industry, palladium is also used to make jewelry and watches, to make blood sugar test strips, surgical instruments, aircraft spark plugs, electrical contacts, surgical instruments, and professional transverse flutes. Since all of these uses are full-fledged industries, the world relies on the supply of palladium. This means that it is a precious metal that is in high demand. The demand for palladium is expected to increase even more in the future, especially because it has become a popular trend on the jewelry market for men in addition to platinum.

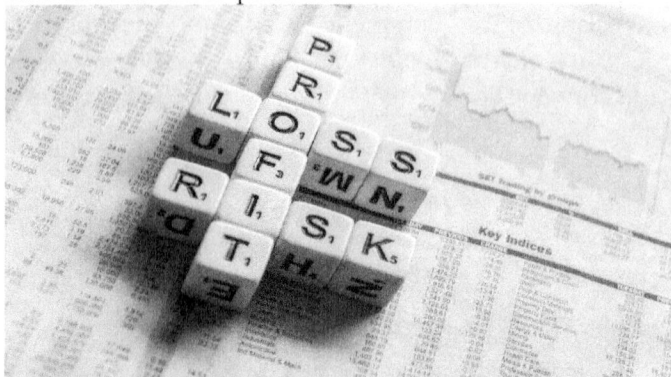

Advantages

Palladium has a naturally bright 'white' color. Although it looks similar to white gold, the two differ because white gold tends to fade with time or may require re-plating after a while. Since palladium's color quality lasts forever, it's often preferred over white gold. The precious metal also has a similar look and resistance as platinum but doesn't cost as much, which means that jewelers often favor palladium over white gold and platinum even though all three metals are used to construct jewelry.

Due to its durability, palladium is used to mold all sorts of accessories on the jewelry market, especially for men's rings, bracelets, chains, belts, and watches. The precious metal has made a name for itself in the fashion industry for men as a key element to accessorize with, which obviously means that more people are purchasing it than ever before. This results in very high demand, especially in combination with other industries that make use of palladium.

Another reason that jewelers favor palladium is that it isn't too heavy. In fact, it weighs about the same as gold. Containing similar properties, it is also malleable, which makes it easier to shape and design compared to other precious metals. Apart from this, the metal also doesn't contain any nickel, which means that it is an ideal option for people that have allergies.

If you're wondering whether there are any other differences between palladium and its sister precious metal, platinum, indeed they do look a bit different. Palladium has a very attractive silver-white sheen and is darker than platinum. Even though this is the case, however, they look very similar to the naked eye and almost identical at a quick glance. Given that palladium is slightly harder than platinum, it is more durable and used to be more affordable until the demand for it increased. Its permanent color appeal makes it a very popular option for anyone that would like to mold it into a product.

Disadvantages

Although the lighter weight of palladium can serve as an advantage, some people have different preferences and prefer a heavier metal for certain jewelry pieces, especially engagement rings and wedding bands. The fact that palladium arrived a little late to the precious metal party may also affect how well it does compared to other precious metals in the jewelry market, as it is uncertain whether the metal is just a part of another trend or will be in fashion longer.

While palladium is a good short-term investment, due to the unpredictability of the markets, one can never be too sure whether its value will last. This is both because it's new to the scene of many industries, but also because of its rarity, which is 15 times rarer than platinum and 30 times rarer than gold. For this reason, even though it is favored as a good quality metal for wedding rings, it's still not a common wedding band metal due to its limited supply. Due to the metal's unique set of characteristics that are different from both gold and platinum, it's also quite difficult to resize, especially because not many jewelers work with it regularly.

Palladium vs. Gold

In February 2021, palladium's price reached a high of $3,000 per ounce, while the gold price was $1,734.60 per ounce. That is a massive difference and means that palladium is much more valuable and profitable than gold, in part because of its rarity. So, if palladium is more valuable than gold, then why doesn't everybody jump at the opportunity to invest in it? Well, that's because it's not a matter of why not, but more because there is not enough palladium available for every trader to make a decent profit off it.

The industrial demand for both palladium and gold is quite high, yet that of palladium is higher than gold. One industry that makes particular use of large quantities of palladium is the auto industry, which uses it primarily for catalytic converters of vehicles. This industry accounts for most of the demand for palladium, making it one of the key positive influencing factors contributing to ever-increasing palladium prices. On the other side, as palladium gets exposed to the auto industry's strong demand, it can also lead to price fluctuation and volatility that is much greater than that of gold. As a result, palladium can be considered less conservative than gold.

Since the auto industry is busy converting to a future in fully electric vehicles (EVs) which make no emissions, this will decrease the need for catalytic converters and thus the need for such large quantities of palladium. Now, before you think that this is a bad thing for investing in palladium, it's not. Since the need for palladium won't be as high as it is now in the auto industry, the vast use of the precious metal will reduce, which will allow investors to invest in more palladium than before due to increased availability.

Trading Profitability

With its massive automobile and investment demand, constrained supply which can lead to rising prices, and ability to build portfolio diversification, there is more than just one reason why trading can be beneficial for anyone. To invest in palladium means to bet on the continuously rising demand for automobiles in countries that continue to grow, like China and India.

Since both Europe and the United States have low interest rates, buying automobiles from China and India benefits these two leading nations, which is why palladium continues to maintain its popularity. Since these automobiles can be bought at much lower rates than vehicles that are made in certain countries like Germany or Italy, people gain more affordable access to credit markets. With most buyers financing automobile purchases, the rates of automobiles made in China and India play a significant role in determining palladium's demand.

With three-quarters of the world's precious metals supply only coming from South Africa and Russia, you can guess who the largest importer of palladium is. That's right, it's the United States. The history of tension between the US and Russia could be a factor that impacts palladium's trading profitability, as if Russia curtails its palladium exports the price of palladium will increase. This will make it less likely for the automobile and retail industry to purchase palladium at the scale that they usually do.

Now, you may be thinking, if that happens, at least South Africa is still in the mix to ensure that the prices of palladium remain stable, right? Well, if you know anything about the southernmost African country, you may have heard just how fragile it is. Due to the country's labor disputes, mining regulations, and political and economic turmoil, the price of palladium could also rise as a result.

When it comes to portfolio diversification with palladium, most investors hold their assets in stocks and bonds. Acting as a commodity, palladium provides a way to diversify and reduce the risk of portfolios. Portfolio diversification improves your likeliness of trading like a pro, which improves your trading profitability, but it also ensures that you are not risking your capital.

By diversifying your portfolio, you can keep any single one of your investment assets from carrying too much weight. This makes it more likely for you to profit, rather than take a loss if a single asset does not perform as expected. With this, you will minimize the risk of any potential losses to your portfolio as a whole, be exposed to a greater pool of opportunities for return and be safeguarded against adverse market cycles.

The PGM market contains precious metals that are all very important in trading and investing. Including platinum, palladium, ruthenium, iridium, rhodium, and osmium, all of which are extremely rare, the group of metals only account for 0.0005 per million of the crust of the Earth. This rarity is the key reason why it is considered a good move to add any of these precious metals to your investment portfolio. With superior catalytic features, especially the malleability of all PGMs, it is no wonder why more and more traders want to start trading with them.

Buying Palladium Jewelry as an Investment

When it comes to investing in jewelry, your safest bet is to invest in palladium. That's because gold, white gold specifically, tends to discolor over time, losing its yellow color. While some people barely notice it, others take the discoloration factor quite seriously, which is why many prefer palladium.

The engagement and wedding supply industry are massive key players in the jewelry market globally, and the good news is that many of them recognize palladium as one of the best precious metals to develop a long-lasting product. Not only do people like to buy palladium, especially as men's accessories or engagement and wedding rings, but the precious metal has also left a mark on massive jewelry retailers who are aware of how valuable it is.

Due to its rarity, palladium is often compared with gold, which even though gold is also rare, it's far from the rarity level of palladium. If you invest in palladium over gold or any other precious metal, you can expect gradual and consistent growth with time. Since gold and palladium are both used to design and manufacture jewelry, there is always some competition in the market between the two. This is why you can trade with either precious metal successfully.

Just like gold, palladium can be bought as an investment by simply purchasing a piece of jewelry that contains it. This means you are buying palladium physically. You can also buy it in larger quantities on trading platforms, all of which will be in its physical form, which means you will have to store it for safety purposes or until you resell it at a more profitable price.

Due to its many monetary benefits, palladium is considered a store of wealth that holds a lot of investment potential. If you're set on making some money but are new at investments, then buying palladium rings or other pieces of jewelry is a great way to go. It's a good alternative to palladium stocks, ETFs, and bullion, all of which are also very profitable options. Due to its rarity, you will always be able to find a broker to buy the jewelry from you in the future.

Palladium Mining Stocks

Palladium mining stocks are very valuable investment because of palladium's rarity and many uses. Since there isn't that much palladium to work with in the world, any form you buy it in is considered an investment.

Palladium is among the most expensive precious metals to invest in compared to the other three, including gold, silver, and platinum. Apart from its rarity, palladium is also very difficult to extract from the earth. Since it is limited and has a high price, there are no dedicated miners for it. As a result, it is considered to be a secondary byproduct of digging for any other precious metals. With this in mind, you can think of palladium as a precious metal mined by accident, which sounds silly considering how valuable it is.

Trading palladium mining stocks is a good way to diversify your investment portfolio. By trading, you are speculating on palladium's share price which will either rise or fall. This also affects the price of leveraged derivatives, such as CFDs. When you trade palladium mining stocks, consider using leverage to increase your exposure, but keep in mind that this will magnify both profits and losses.

The top palladium stocks to invest in include:

- Norilsk Nickel
- Sibanye-Stillwater
- Anglo American Platinum
- Impala Platinum
- Northam Platinum

Aberdeen Standard Physical Palladium Shares ETF

The purpose of the palladium ETFs is to track the price of palladium at any point in time. As of 2021, the Physical Palladium Standard Shares fund (PALL) is the only palladium ETF that exists in the U.S. markets. Therefore, this palladium ETF manages the total palladium assets, which come in at $461.77 million. The palladium ETF is categorized under the commodities asset class.

With an increasing demand for palladium in the automotive and jewelry industry, the price of palladium reached an all-time high of $2,909.30 per ounce at the end of April 2021. With this price, the gold-palladium ratio has decreased, favoring palladium which now trades higher than gold.

With prices continuing to rise, the Aberdeen Standard Physical Palladium Shares ETF (PALL) is incredibly well-positioned to deliver proper returns. PALL reflects the performance of palladium's price and is designed for investors that are seeking a convenient and cost-effective method to invest in the precious metal without the presence of credit risk.

As it stands, PALL has $477.50 million in Assets Under Management (AUM) in 2021. Although its 0.60% expense ratio is higher than the 0.49% category average, the ETF has managed to rise in price by 42.6% in over just a year. With 30.6% of this increase occurring over a recent period of 9 months. Thus far, ETF net inflows have generated $32.24 million in a single month, which displays just how profitable a palladium shares ETF investment can be. With a promising outlook, the ETF has an A grade that equates to a Strong Buy rating in the stock market. It also ranks in the top five within the category of precious metals ETFs, lending further credit to its profitability.

Chapter 4: How to Start Trading PGM Like a Pro

When you invest in a single or more than one Platinum Group Metal (PGM), you must review their prices. While your first instinct to the pricing of metals, much like anything else, could be that if it has the lowest price it is better to invest in it, think again. What you should be looking for is something that has potential, which means a commodity with a high price. Currently, rhodium, platinum, palladium, and iridium are among the top, most expensive metals to invest in, similar to gold.

To understand how to start trading as a beginner, you must understand the difference between a bull and bear market. A bull market is on the rise, growing, and economically sound, while bear markets sing a different tune. Bear markets refer to markets that recede and usually involve stocks that are declining in value.

When looking at an expensive PGM to invest in, don't think that you're in way over your head when it comes to the price. Consider an expensive precious metal in your possession as a valuable asset. Precious metals like PGMs offer very high liquidity and provide you with excellent opportunities to make a profit from many different environments, mainly due to their position in the world's political and economic systems.

Even if investing in precious metals can be expensive compared to other commodities, when you invest in PGMs, gold, or even silver, you are gaining leverage with measured risk, which means that it is one of the safest investments you could make.

When you start trading with PGMs, compared to more lucrative precious metals, like gold and silver which every trader or investment professional seems to have an opinion about, it's not quite the same thing. Even though PGMs are in high demand for various types of industries, most people remain unaware of how promising it can be to invest in these underrated metals.

Highly valued in the jewelry production and the automobile industry, palladium has been classified as a commodity that is necessary for certain industries to function optimally. After all, the use of palladium in catalytic converters allows the automobile industry to decrease harmful emissions and meet regulatory standards. Since some of the biggest nations in the world are moving towards a greener initiative, it's no doubt why palladium, next to the four other PGMs, is valued as much as it is.

The use of palladium in catalytic converters has been on the rise since 1989. However, this requires automakers to use over 75% of the 208,000 kilograms of palladium that is mined each year. Palladium is also considered a very valuable metal for nuclear industries as it can absorb up to 900 times its volume in hydrogen (Capital.com, 2019).

Apart from building more eco-friendly cars and making them safer, PGMs are also used to treat cancer. This is especially relevant for platinum, which can slow down or stop the division of living cells in the human body. As a result, biochemists have created platinum-based drugs to treat many different types of cancers. PGMs also help people maintain personal hygiene, as platinum-cured mixtures are integrated into many personal care products today, including contact lenses, lipsticks, and shampoos.

PGMs even help keep us warm as they're used in the manufacturing of synthetic rubber, plastics, and polyester fibers to produce blankets and clothes. Palladium helps maintain food freshness due to a high-tech palladium-containing sheet that gets placed at the bottom of fruit and vegetable packaging, and platinum fuel-based cells provide power off-grid.

Getting an even bigger idea of how broad the PGM market is and all the things it is essential for and required for in our everyday lives, not just in one country, but every country in the world puts the significance of trading with it in perspective. Quite frankly, it's one of the best investments that you can make.

If you are interested in trading with PGMs and adding them to your long-term investment portfolio, there are four steps to get started, but first, you must grasp the fundamentals that affect the price of PGMs. This should give you a long-term perspective on the price of each type of metal. Once you have done this, you must then do adequate research on market psychology and how traders think. This will allow you to recognize what their next potential move could be.

For a successful beginner trading experience, follow these four steps:

Step 1: Understand what moves PGMs

The Platinum Group Metals market is set to register a compound annual growth rate (CAGR) of more than 4.5% amid the forecast period between 2021 and 2026. In 2020, the market was significantly impacted by Covid-19 in a very negative way.

Since many countries were forced into lockdown, the demand from the automotive catalyst industry declined. However, the demand for electrodes made from PGMs in blood gas analyzers and platinum catalysts for the production of medical-grade and polypropylene silicones for personal protective equipment (PPE) manufacturing, along with PGM metal catalysts used to produce active pharmaceutical ingredients (API's) for antibiotics, has increased as a result of the pandemic. This has stimulated the market demand for PGMs.

Before the Covid-19 pandemic, the automobile catalyst industry required most of the PGMs mined in the world, but now, it's a different story. Platinum, palladium, and ruthenium demand continues to grow as a result, yet the pandemic is set to continue hindering market growth for the next couple of years post-2020. This is mainly due to the high costs of maintenance of these metals and the impact of the pandemic.

Currently, research and development (R&D) activities for the application of PGMs within the electronics sector and the trend of increasing investments in African countries are what will be the PGM market's saving grace for years to come. This market is expected to be dominated by the Asia-Pacific region which is predicted to see the highest CAGR amid the forecast period. This region has accounted for the biggest market share for PGMs and owns nearly half of the global share thus far, which is expected to become the fastest-growing market. With China being one of the biggest holders that accounts for almost 50% of the regional market share, the demand for PGMs in petroleum and chemical refining applications will continue to benefit from investments in China's big integrated petrochemical complexes.

Since China is the largest hard drive disk producer globally, they have also managed to create an incredibly big demand for PGMs that impacts the entire world. With Japan's high demand for platinum jewelry and South Korea presenting a brand-new growth market in fuel technology, the increasing demand helps to drive a bull market in PGM trading, despite the market effects of Covid-19.

Providing a competitive landscape, the PGM market is considered highly consolidated. Five key players account for a major share in the market, which includes:

- Anglo American Platinum

- Impala Platinum Holdings Limited
- Sibanye-Stillwater
- Northam Platinum Limited
- PJSC MMC Norilsk Nickel

These key players are responsible for providing complete resource-to-market services to a global customer network with a variety of mined, traded, and recycled products.

Just like with other precious metals, the volume and trend intensity of PGMs are affected by inflation and deflation, greed and fear, and supply and demand.

Thanks to such high demand, even with the presence of Covid-19 post-2020, PGM prices continue to soar, presenting great promise for its future and that of any person who has invested in precious metals. PGMs can be mined and manufactured into just about anything due to their malleability, but they're commonly sold in the form of coins or bars. In both cases, they can be melted and reshaped for the jewelry market, automobile industry, medical industries, and any other industry that finds use for it.

Step 2: Where to find and trade PGMs

Some of the best reasons to invest in PGMs include betting on industrial growth, a weakened US Dollar, or a supply and demand imbalance. Once you understand PGMs, it's time to trade, and yes, you can trade any PGM you like, even as a beginner!

Some of the best broker platforms to trade PGMs include:

1. ForexPro (FxPro)
2. AVATrade
3. CM Trading
4. Plus500
5. ETORO
6. Alpari
7. Fp Markets
8. Forex Time Company (FXTM)

9. easyMarkets
10. Trading212

There are several ways for an investor to invest in one of the five PGMs, which include:

1. Bullion - The complexity rating of bullion is extremely easy, which is a plus point, yet it involves storage costs. It doesn't have an expiration date, management cost, leverage, and is not regulated.

2. CFDs - Contract for Difference (CFD) enables you to speculate on rising or falling prices on global financial markets. This type of PGM investment isn't considered too difficult for the beginner trader but may be a better option to trade with once you've gained experience in trading with platinum bullion, ETF, and shares. It has no storage costs, expiration date, or management cost, it holds leverage, and is regulated.

3. Futures - This investment trading option is very hard to trade with, has no storage cost, has an expiration date, no management cost, has leverage, and is regulated.

4. Options - This investment trading option is also considered very hard to trade with, has no storage cost, has an expiration date, no management cost, has leverage, and is regulated.

5. ETFs - Next to bullion, ETFs are very easy to trade with, include no storage cost, no expiration date, but have a management cost, have no leverage, and are regulated.

6. Shares - This is among the three best options, next to bullion and ETFs, to trade with as it is very easy to do so. It has no storage cost, no expiration date or management cost, has leverage, and is regulated.

Note: Storage costs are required to be paid by traders as management fees.

Step 3: How to trade PGMs

1. Bullions

PGM bullion coins and bars are sold by metal dealers in the same way that gold and silver bullion is sold. In the US, investors can buy, for example, American Platinum Eagle coins with a purity of 99.95%, whereas platinum bars are fabricated at foundries to meet different sizes, including 1 oz, 10 oz, and even 1 kilogram. To buy physical platinum requires you to physically store it, which involves a storage cost for safety deposit boxes or units.

Some of the best and most trustworthy online PGM bullion dealers include:

- JMBullion.com

- BullionVault.com
- APMEX.com
- Moneymetals.com

2. Futures

   The Chicago Mercantile Exchange (CME) and the New York Mercantile Exchange (NYMEX) both offer PGM futures contracts which are derivative products that get traded on the exchange. Investors trading futures utilize leverage to purchase contracts that are tied to the platinum price. Should it decline, investors are required to put up an additional margin to maintain certain positions, as well as roll futures contracts forward monthly, or accept physical delivery of it. Futures investment requires maintenance of positions by the investor.

3. Options

   This type of trading is a derivative instrument, which also trades on the NYMEX. However, unlike futures, options have an expiry date. When you buy options, you pay a premium to the seller, which gets exchanged for the right to use the option in the future. Options traders are required to make correct determinations about the timing and size of a specific PGM price shift to profit from their trades.

4. ETFs

PGM ETFs trade as shares on exchanges just like stocks. There are many ways to invest in PGMs by using exchange-traded funds (ETFs), with the most popular being:

- PPLT (ETFs Physical Platinum Shares)
- PGM (iPath Dow Jones-UBS Platinum ETN)
- SPPP (Sprott Physical Platinum and Palladium Trust)

5. Mining Company Shares

Many publicly traded companies have exposure to Platinum Group Metal prices, and investing in these companies is an ideal way to capitalize on this exposure. Many of the following companies have exposure to these prices, including:

- Anglo Platinum
- Impala Platinum
- Norilsk nickel (Nornickel)

6. CFDs

If you choose to invest in PGMs through the use of contract for difference (CFD) derivative investments, note that CFDs allow investors to only speculate on PGM without buying assets, including bullion, futures, options, ETFs, or mining shares. There are many regulated brokers globally that offer PGM CFDs. With CFDs, traders deposit their funds with a broker that serves as a margin. There are advantages to trading CFDs, which include that the investor gains exposure to PGMs without having to purchase or store bullion or manage complex options or futures positions.

Best Trading Strategies

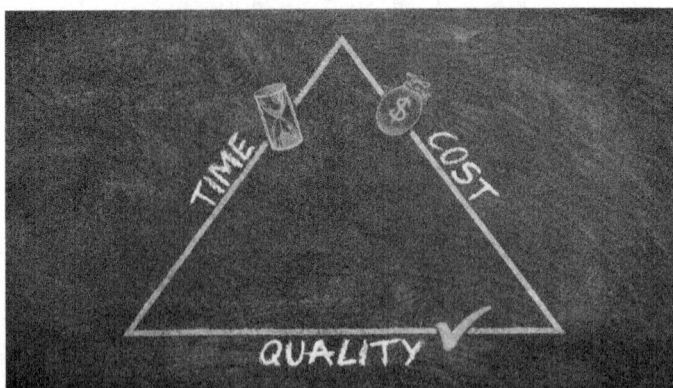

1. News trading

A method of trading that is based on news, but also market expectations before and after news releases. This requires trading on new announcements, which requires one to have a skilled mindset, especially in modern times with news traveling fast on digital media. To do news trading, you must assess the news once it's been released, the more immediate, the better. Once it is released, you must make a judgment on how to trade with your information fast, upon which you must consider whether the news is fully factored into the price or only partially priced, along with if the news matches market expectations.

For a successful news trade, you must understand the differences in market expectations, which will be necessary to achieve success.

When you start:

- Treat every market and news release individually.
- Develop a trading strategy for a specific news release.
- Consider market expectations and reactions, which can be more important than the news releases themselves.

Benefits: News trading offers a more defined entry and exit strategy with many trading opportunities.

2. End-of-day trading

This trading strategy involves, as you can guess, trading near the closing period of markets, which is at the end of the day. This is because traders know that trading prices are going to either settle or close during this time. It requires a strategy of studying price action compared to that of the previous day's price movements. With this type of trading, one can speculate how the prices will move based on price action, and then decide on the indicators used in the system. To avoid risks, traders must create a risk management order, a limit-order, a stop-loss order, as well as a take-profit order.

This type of trading requires time, more so than other trading strategies because you have to study charts during opening and closing times.

Benefits: End-of-day trading is suitable for most traders and requires a smaller time commitment because it only operates at night.

3. Swing trading

As the third type of trading, swing trading refers to both movement sides of a financial market. Swing traders aim to purchase a security whenever they expect the market to rise. Alternatively, they aim to sell assets when they suspect that the price is set to fall. Swing trading takes advantage of the market's oscillations, with the price fluctuating regularly from an overbought to an oversold state. This type of trading is a technical approach to analyzing markets that is achieved through studying charts and analyzing the individual movements that affect a bigger-picture trend.

To become a successful swing trader, you must be able to interpret the length and duration of every swing, which defines significant support and resistance levels. Swing traders also need to be able to identify trends that involve markets encountering increasing levels of both supply and demand.

Here are some tips for getting started:

- With strong trends, note that you can use retracement swings to enter a direction of a specific trend. Such points are referred to as 'pullbacks' or 'dips'.
- When a momentum high occurs, look at the highest probability trade, which means buying the first pullback.
- Use a pattern recognition scanner. It will help you identify chart patterns to aid in technical analysis.

Benefits: Swing trading can be practiced as a hobby, which means that it doesn't take up too much time. It also offers a variety of trade opportunities.

4. Day trading

This type of trading is also known as intra-day trading and is suitable for anyone that wants to actively trade during the day, perhaps even as a full-time profession. Day traders value price fluctuations during the market's open and closed hours and generally hold multiple positions open during the day. However, they don't leave positions open during the night, as this minimizes the potential risks of overnight market volatility. For the best day trading experience, one must follow an organized trading plan that is adaptable to fast-paced market movements.

Note: Before the markets open for day trading, traders must study support and resistance levels, along with possible reactions to a previous night's US trading markets. Following this step, trade on the European markets for the first two hours during a high liquidity period, or between 12 p.m. and 5 p.m. GMT when both the US and UK markets are open.

Benefits: Day trading doesn't involve overnight risk like with end-of-day trading. It has a limited intraday risk because trades only last between one to four hours, minimizing the risks of longer-term trades. This type of trading offers time flexibility as it is during the day for a short duration, along with multiple trade opportunities on the international markets.

5. Trend trading

A type of trading that involves traders using technical analysis to define a trend, which enters trades in the direction of a predetermined trend. This type of trading isn't dependent on bullish or bearish markets but can be defined by the presence of an accurate system that is set in place to determine and follow trends. With this type of trading, it is necessary to remain alert and be adaptable as trends can change quickly. One thing trend traders should remain aware of is the risks of market reversals that are mitigated with trailing stop-loss orders.

Many trend-following tools can be utilized for analyzing markets that include equities, commodities, currencies, and treasuries. Trend trading requires the patience and discipline to follow their rules. If ever your system stops working due to a fundamental market change, you must cut your losses short and only let profits run during trend trading.

When you start:

- Remain alert for trends that are ending or are set to change, and note that the last part of a trend can accelerate when traders with the wrong positions want to cut losses.

- Decide on a timeframe to follow the trend and keep it consistent.

Benefits: Trend trading is a useful hobby because it is perfect for anyone that wants to earn money on the side but has limited time. It also offers many trading opportunities that allow you to enter and exit trades.

Chapter 5: Bonus - Investing Tips on Rhodium

Rhodium is one of the lesser known, but impressive PGMs, next to platinum and palladium, both of which are considered very successful in the world of trading. However, just because there aren't as many people talking about rhodium does not mean that it's not a promising investment. Rhodium is considered one of the most popular metals to trade.

Its popularity began with a 30% price surge at the start of 2020 and has continued to grow thereafter. This comes after a peak in 2008 that pushed the price of rhodium to over $10,000 per troy ounce (t oz), which was considered to be a lot at the time. Today, in May 2021, the metal trades at $29,000 t oz, which continues to grow gradually over time. Given that rhodium has just about tripled in value in just over ten years, the precious metal holds a lot of promise for the future (Intelligent HQ, n.d.).

Like palladium, rhodium is used to construct catalytic converters, which is the part of a vehicle's exhaust system responsible for reducing toxic gas emissions and pollutants. According to S&P Global Platts, like with palladium, nearly 80% of rhodium demand comes from the automotive industry. The metal is rarer than platinum and palladium, and has an annual production of 30 tons, in comparison to gold miners which produce up to 3,000 tons a year (Intelligent HQ, n.d.).

Any investor who has kept his or her eye on PGMs knows that rhodium is one precious metal to invest money in. Given that the rhodium market is relatively small apart from its usage in the automotive industry, there are few ways to purchase it. The best way to do so is by buying physical rhodium bullion, such as coins and bars. Some popular coins made of rhodium include the $100 Rhodium Tuvalu coin, which is the world's first coin made from 100% rhodium. Only 1,000 Rhodium Tuvalu coins were made, and each consists of 1 oz of rhodium.

Alternatively, you can opt for the Baird & Co. .999 pure 1 oz rhodium bar or the 1 oz PAMP Suisse Lady Fortuna bar, both of which are manufactured by reputable companies, are encased in protective holders, and have a serial number for investors to rest assured about the coins' or bars' validity. Before purchasing coins or bars, one must always check the fine detail on them to ensure it is the real deal (Intelligent HQ, n.d.).

These coins and bars are good investments because they only contain a small premium over the spot price, are small and lightweight, which makes them easy to store and ship, and don't require much storage space.

Alternatively to physical bullion, more ways to invest in rhodium include trading with the DWS rhodium ETF, which delivered a 194% return in just 12 months. Rhodium coins can additionally be bought as a virtual currency and be secured in a vault, which can be redeemed by buyers through digital holdings at any time.

Apart from diversifying your investment portfolio, investing in rhodium is a very unique way to invest in a valuable and rare precious metal that continues to grow in value with rising demand (Intelligent HQ, n.d.).

Conclusion

The future of Platinum Group Metals (PGMs) is brighter than most people may think, and as you embark on a journey to navigate the precious metals market, it's important to keep track of the cost of PGMs. While they are expensive compared to many popular precious metals, the supply and demand of PGMs are also two key factors to keep in mind when you decide to invest in them. With increasing prices surging since 2019, it is far more meaningful that traders understand what drives market conditions, along with what one can expect going forward.

Since the world is slowly but surely moving towards a greener initiative, precious metals like platinum, palladium, and rhodium are all considered very useful in the automotive industry going forward. Currently, these precious metals are trending upward and will continue to do so in the future as they are valued for their impressive characteristics. Given the fact that automakers are now being forced to comply with tightening their emissions standards, more so in China and Europe, the demand for metals will continue to grow which can create a big and successful investment for your future.

From learning more about platinum, palladium, rhodium, and how they compare to gold, along with their place in the markets, there is much to learn about what may be considered the runt of the litter next to some of the biggest precious metals out there today. With hopeful trading profitability, you can follow some of the most constructive strategies to start as a successful beginner trader.

References

AllBusiness Editors. (2018, September 23). *Top 10 Reasons to Invest Your Money | AllBusiness.com*. AllBusiness.com. https://www.allbusiness.com/top-10-reasons-to-invest-money-93916-1.html

27+ Best Regulated Forex Brokers - (Reviewed and Compared). (2021, January 8). SA Shares. https://sashares.co.za/best-forex-regulated-brokers/#gs.052r37

Brock, Thomas, (2021, March 14). *A Beginner's Guide to Precious Metals*. (2019). Investopedia. https://www.investopedia.com/articles/basics/09/precious-metals-gold-silver-platinum.asp

(2021, October 25). Capital.com. https://capital.com/trade-palladium

Everything You Ever Wanted to Know About Palladium - Buy & Sell Gold & Silver Wisely in Denver, CO | Rocky Mountain Coin. (2015, May 22). Buy & Sell Gold & Silver Wisely in Denver, CO | Rocky Mountain Coin.

https://rmcoin.com/palladium/everything-you-ever-wanted-to-know-about-palladium/

Farley, Alan. (2021, March 13). https://www.investopedia.com/articles/investing/100915/learn-how-trade-gold-4-steps.asp

Find out about the advantages and disadvantages of Platinum 950 | Quality Diamonds. (n.d.). Www.qualitydiamonds.co.uk. https://www.qualitydiamonds.co.uk/expert-advice/buying-guides/choosing-your-setting-metal/platinum-950/

Fried, Michael. (2021, April 19). *Palladium Vs Platinum Wedding Rings | All the Pros & Cons.* (n.d.). The Diamond Pro. Retrieved April 27, 2021, from https://www.diamonds.pro/education/palladium-vs-platinum-wedding-bands/

Gallagher, Anthony. (2021, May 1). https://www.securities.io/gold-vs-palladium-key-differences-for-investors/

Glaister, Bonnie., and Mudd, Gavin. (2010, April). *The environmental costs of platinum–PGM mining and sustainability: Is the glass half-full or half-empty? | Request PDF.* (n.d.). ResearchGate. https://www.researchgate.net/publication/223232620_The_environmental_costs_of_platinum_

PGM mining and sustainability Is the glass half-full or half-empty

Helmenstine, Ph.D., Anne Marie. (2019, July 2). *A List of Precious Metals and What Makes Them Valuable*. ThoughtCo. https://www.thoughtco.com/list-of-precious-metals-608467

Himmatramka, Krish. (2015, March 29). *Gold vs Platinum | What's the Best Metal for Your Ring*. (2015, March 29). Do Amore. https://www.doamore.com/gold-vs-platinum-metal-for-your-ring/

Images sourced from www.freeimages.com

Images sourced from www.pixabay.com

Investing in Palladium | Is Palladium a Good Investment? (2019). Www.monex.com. https://www.monex.com/investing-in-palladium/

Investing in PGM. (n.d.). *Www.sharpspixley.com*. Retrieved April 14, 2021, from https://www.sharpspixley.com/guide/invest-in-pgm

Investing in PGMs. (n.d.). *Www.sharpspixley.com*. Retrieved May 6, 2021, from https://www.sharpspixley.com/investment-guide/investing-in-pgms

3 Key Trends In Palladium Trading For 2021 – Including Insight On Chinese Demand. (2021, February 26).

Commodity.com. Retrieved May 6, 2021, from https://commodity.com/precious-metals/palladium/trading/

More precious than gold: Why palladium is soaring. (2020, January 20). *BBC News*. https://www.bbc.com/news/business-51171391

Palladium - Element information, properties and uses | *Periodic Table. (2011). Rsc.org. https://www.rsc.org/periodic-table/element/46/palladium*

Palladium Prices Today | Live Spot Palladium Price per Ounce. *(2019). Www.monex.com. https://www.monex.com/palladium-prices/*

Platinum. (2014, September 23). Chemicool.com. https://www.chemicool.com/elements/platinum.html

Platinum-Group Element - an overview | ScienceDirect Topics. (n.d.). Www.sciencedirect.com. https://www.sciencedirect.com/topics/materials-science/platinum-group-element

Platinum Group Metals Market | Growth, Trends, COVID-19 Impact, and Forecasts (2021 - 2026). (n.d.). Www.mordorintelligence.com. https://www.mordorintelligence.com/industry-reports/platinum-group-metals-market

Platinum Trading In 2021: Is It A More Affordable Precious Metal Investment Than Gold? (2021, January 29).

Commodity.com.
https://commodity.com/precious-metals/platinum/trading/

Pines, Lawrence. (2021, January 29).
https://commodity.com/precious-metals/palladium/trading/

Pines, Lawrence. (2021, January 29). *Platinum Trading In 2021: Is It A More Affordable Precious Metal Investment Than Gold?* (n.d.). Commodity.com. Retrieved April 17, 2021, from https://commodity.com/precious-metals/platinum/trading/

Rand, Steve. (2020, January 31). *Platinum Price Forecast 2020.* (2020, January 31). Scottsdale Bullion & Coin.
https://www.sbcgold.com/blog/platinum-price-forecast-2020/

Ross, Rachel. (2016, August 1). Facts About Platinum. *Live Science; Live Science.* https://www.livescience.com/39144-platinum.html

Stewart, Alex. G. (2019, July 9). *Mining is bad for health: a voyage of discovery. Environmental Geochemistry and Health.* https://doi.org/10.1007/s10653-019-00367-7

6 Trading Strategies Every Trader Should Know | CMC Markets. (n.d.). Www.cmcmarkets.com.

https://www.cmcmarkets.com/en/trading-guides/trading-strategies

The Assay. (n.d.). *A Long and Winding Road: The Future of Platinum Group Metals.* (2019, December 10). The Assay. https://www.theassay.com/articles/a-long-and-winding-road-the-future-of-platinum-group-metals/

The five most expensive metals and where they are mined. (2020, March 10). Www.mining-Technology.com. Retrieved May 6, 2021, from https://www.mining-technology.com/features/five-most-expensive-metals-and-where-they-are-mined/

Seven unexpected uses of Platinum Group Metals (PGMs). (2015, August 13). *Www.angloamerican.com. Retrieved May 6, 2021, from https://www.angloamerican.com/about-us/our-stories/seven-unexpected-uses-of-pgms*

What are CFDs? | CFD Trading Meaning | CMC Markets. (n.d.). *Www.cmcmarkets.com. Retrieved May 6, 2021, from https://www.cmcmarkets.com/en/learn-cfd-trading/what-are-cfds*

What are the advantages and disadvantages of platinum? (2018). - *Brainly.in.* Brainly.in. https://brainly.in/question/7016339

World Platinum Investment Council - Investment Research - Platinum Perspectives. (n.d.).

Platinuminvestment.com. Retrieved April 17, 2021, from https://platinuminvestment.com/investment-research/perspectives

About the Author

M. L. Pilgrim lost millions when he was starting as an entrepreneur but only his consistent belief in the power of the subconscious mind has brought him to his success. He is very active investing with majority of his portfolio in precious metals and stocks. Also, he invests in bonds, mutual funds, UITFs, and in other businesses in real estate, power generation, banking, logistics, retail, and telecommunications.

He worked across 10 countries always fascinated with the beauty of nature, culture, and traditions. He is a versatile author writing both fiction and non-fiction. He is a traveler, a dedicated father, a loving son, and a responsible brother.

He strongly believes that everyone can succeed both in business, relationships, society, and other aspects if they only have the right information and knowledge on how to use that information properly.

M. L. Pilgrim uses a pen name as he doesn't want to show himself as a definitive expert. Instead, he is in this journey with his readers like a "pilgrim" and wants to travel with them and share their experiences.

Reach M. L. Pilgrim in mlpilgrim.author@gmail.com. Cheers!

Or subscribe to his newsletter for latest updates on his investment books.

Books by This Author

THE PEOPLE'S GOLD: EVERYONE, EVERYWHERE, EVERY TIME! A Beginner's Practical Guide on All You Need to Know on How to Profit from Gold

Don't have gold in your investment portfolio? Here's why you're missing out.

Is gold just for the rich?

Is it irrelevant in this highly digital economy?

Will it be of any use to your already diversified portfolio?

With prices at thousands of dollars for a few grams, gold is an expensive element.

You'd have good reason to believe that it's only something the wealthy would buy, and probably just as a part of their collection of expensive things.

But gold is much more than a material for luxurious jewelry or for ornate decorations.

Nowadays, gold is considered a safe haven for investors in an increasingly volatile market.

Some investors invest in gold when they foresee a recession, inflation, or uncertainty. Others hold on to gold to preserve wealth, while having a vehicle to pass it on to future generations.

In short, because uncertainty is inherent in any investment and in any economy, gold can serve as insurance in case of economic or political disasters.

Even in a highly digitized economy, gold continues to be attractive because it's a tangible asset that can still be of value, even if our entire monetary system collapses.

Fortunately, gone are the days when you had to pan for gold in a river, under the heat of the sun, with the possibility of ending up with nothing but a severe sunburn.

In today's economy, gold is easier to access and more affordable as well.

There are several ways to invest in gold that require nothing more than a computer, an internet connection, and a reasonable amount of money.

Don't lose out on the benefits of gold in your portfolio, even if you don't have billions of dollars to spare.

In THE PEOPLE'S GOLD: EVERYONE, EVERYWHERE, EVERY TIME!, YOU WILL DISCOVER:

- A **step-by-step guide** to getting started with gold investments, which you can follow even without any investing background
- How to legitimately invest in gold with **less than $100**
- **How much of your portfolio to invest in gold** so you don't lose out on market gains, but

you still protect yourself enough in case of a
severe downturn

- An **easy and accessible way to invest** in gold
  without having to worry about storage and theft
- How to tell real versus fake gold, and other smart
  ways to **protect yourself from gold scammers**
- Have a better understanding of your profile as a
  gold investor
- The varying reasons for investing in gold, and
  how they affect your investment strategy
- Know the different types of gold investors and
  see which one you can identify yourself the most
- **Bonus chapter**: Practical tips for investing in
  silver that could augment your portfolio even
  more

AND MUCH MORE.

Whether you think the economy as we know it will collapse in the
foreseeable future, or you're just looking for a hedge against low
interest rates, gold offers you this protection and more.

Even if you think your portfolio is already diversified enough, with
stocks, bonds, real estate, and more, gold can still make a valuable
addition to your portfolio.

Its unique qualities & ability to hedge against both equities & fixed
income securities offer an extra layer of diversification &
protection, specially for the most extreme cases.

Don't wait until the economic system collapses. Get some gold
now and ensure that you're financially protected in case anything
ever happens.

If you want to protect your finances & prepare for an uncertain
future with a tangible, safe, & reliable asset, then grab a copy right
now!

EL ORO DE LA GENTE: ¡para todos, en todas partes, en todo momento! Sección extra: cómo vender plata

D¿No tienes oro en tu cartera de inversiones? Te proporcionamos la explicación de por qué te lo estás perdiendo.

¿Es el oro solo para los ricos?

¿Es irrelevante en esta economía tan digital?

¿Será útil para tu cartera de inversiones ya diversificada?

Con precios de miles de dólares por unos pocos gramos, el oro es un elemento caro.

Tendrías buenas razones para creer que es algo que solo comprarían los ricos, y probablemente solo como parte de su colección de cosas caras.

Pero el oro es mucho más que un material para joyas lujosas o para decoraciones ornamentales.

Hoy en día, el oro se considera un refugio seguro para los inversores en un mercado cada vez más volátil.

Algunos inversores invierten en oro cuando prevén una recesión, inflación o incertidumbre. Otros se aferran al oro para preservar su riqueza y tener un vehículo para transmitirla a las generaciones futuras.

I En resumen, dado que la incertidumbre es inherente a cualquier inversión y a cualquier economía, el oro puede servir de seguro en caso de desastres económicos o políticos.

Incluso en una economía altamente digitalizada, el oro sigue siendo atractivo porque es un activo tangible que puede seguir teniendo valor, incluso si todo nuestro sistema monetario se derrumba.

Afortunadamente, ya han pasado los días en los que había que buscar oro en un río, bajo el calor del sol, con la posibilidad de acabar solo con una grave quemadura solar.

En la economía actual, el oro es más fácil de conseguir y también más asequible.

Hay varias formas de invertir en oro que no requieren más que un ordenador, una conexión a Internet y una cantidad razonable de dinero.

No te pierdas las ventajas del oro en tu cartera de inversiones, aunque no tengas miles de millones de dólares de sobra.

En *Oro para la clase media*, descubrirás:

- Una **guía de pasos a seguir** sobre cómo comenzar a invertir en oro, que puedes seguir incluso sin ningún tipo de experiencia en inversiones.
- Cómo invertir legítimamente en oro >con menos de 100 dólares
- Por qué **necesitas comprar oro físico** si estás invirtiendo en oro por esta razón
- **Cuánto de tu cartera de inversiones debes gastar en oro** para no perder las ganancias del mercado, pero aún así protegerte lo suficiente en caso de una recesión severa.
- Una **forma fácil y accesible de invertir** en oro sin que tengas que

preocuparte por su almacenamiento y posible robo.

- Cómo distinguir el oro auténtico del falso, y otras estrategias inteligentes **que te permitirán protegerte de los estafadores de oro.**
- Las diferentes razones para invertir en oro y la manera en que estas afectan tu estrategia de inversión
- **Capítulo extra:**consejos prácticos para invertir en plata que podrían aumentar aún más tu cartera de inversiones.

Y mucho mas.

Ya sea que pienses que la economía tal como la conocemos colapsará en el futuro próximo, o simplemente estás buscando una cobertura contra las bajas tasas de interés, el oro te ofrece esta protección y más.

Incluso si crees que tu cartera de inversiones ya está lo suficientemente diversificada, con acciones, bonos, bienes raíces y demás, el oro aún puede ser una valiosa adición a tu cartera.

Sus cualidades únicas y su capacidad para protegerte tanto de la renta variable como de la renta fija ofrecen una capa adicional de diversificación y protección, especialmente para los casos más extremos.

No esperes a que el sistema económico colapse. Obtén algo de oro ahora y asegúrate de estar protegido financieramente en caso de que algo suceda.

Si quieres proteger tus finanzas y prepararte para un futuro incierto con un activo tangible, seguro y fiable, desplázate hacia arriba y haz clic en el botón "Añadir a la cesta" ahora mismo.

BEST WAYS TO INVEST IN SILVER FOR BEGINNERS (BONUS: NICE FEW TIPS AND WARNINGS ON INVESTING IN SILVER)

What do you know about investing in Silver?

The decision to start a project or take the first steps in the path of investment may be difficult but choosing the right investment and the field that matches your ambitions and needs is much more difficult. Perhaps this fear comes from the idea that you are here at risk of loss. You can easily lose everything that you have gathered in your life, but there is always light in the midst of all this.

Silver is not very much traded in the world, but because people love imitation. "See, this person has succeeded in trading gold, let's be gold traders like him." This is the main reason for loss. Success stories and money of others tempt you, so you start running towards it without awareness even though there are hundreds of fields to choose from.

In this book, we will show you the most important points, methods, strategies, and tips that will give you the best start as a silver trader.

Outlined among the chapters of this book, you will learn about silver investing across the following topics:

√ **Advantages** of Trading in Silver

√ **Disadvantages** of Trading in Silver

√ Is trading in Silver **Profitable**?

√ <u>How to Start</u> the Business?

√ <u>Where to Trade</u> Silver?

√ <u>**Silver Trading Strategies**</u>

We did not write these tips in a night or two and did not discover them by chance, we have already encountered them and have proven their effectiveness, and we have already seen many amazing stories thanks to them and we would like to give you the opportunity to be among them, to use your chances in life!

So, grab a copy now of this book and check out our exciting bonuses and free books that you can avail!

BEST WAYS TO INVEST IN GOLD FOR BEGINNERS: QUICK GUIDE FOR LEARNING AND INVESTING IN GOLD. (BONUS: 14 WAYS TO ESTABLISH REAL GOLD FROM FAKE GOLD AND MORE!)

Gold has kept a great value for thousands of years, and until this day it still occupies this high position, due to its properties that make it at the forefront of precious metals.

As it still retains its value throughout the ages, and the belief that is embedded in people's minds is that gold is the only way to pass and conserve wealth from one generation to another.

In times of political and economic tension as well as natural disasters, investors resort to buying gold as a safe haven in the markets and as a store of value, and it is also used as a hedge against high inflation. If you want gold to be part of your investment portfolio, you can choose from several investment options in gold, each of which has different investment characteristics. In this book, we offer many ways to invest in gold, tips to make the greatest possible start and the guide by which you can avoid fraud. We hope that we could help you, best of luck!

BEST WAYS TO INVEST MONEY DURING COVID-19: MAKE MONEY AT HOME

There are many things we can do during the pandemic and the most productive of all is to invest it wisely. Check out this book for some tips and guidance.

HOW TO UNDERSTAND THE SUBCONSCIOUS MIND: UNLOCK, UNLEASH, AND LET IT TRANSFORM YOU!

What do you know about the subconscious mind?

Do you want to know more about its characteristics? It is within us, but it is elusive in many aspects. So, careful understanding of the subconscious mind will bring us many benefits.

This book will share about the ff:

- What is the subconscious mind?
- Its relationship with the conscious mind
- Methods of connecting with the subconscious mind
- Secrets of the subconscious mind
- The rules of the subconscious mind

- Using your subconscious mind to achieve your goals
- Programming the subconscious mind
- How to achieve sleep miracles
- Controlling your subconscious mind

So, what are you waiting for? Check out this informative yet insightful book in unleashing this mysterious power within ourselves.

HOW TO THRIVE IN AWKWARD CONVERSATIONS: LEARN THE ART OF SPEAKING WITH SKILL AND CONSIDERATION (BONUS! 10 TIPS TO IMPROVE YOUR CONVERSATION SKILLS!)

Have you ever found yourself in the middle of an Awkward Conversation?

Conversation is an art of dealing and communicating with others. Effective Communication aims to build understanding and acceptance - not conflict. However, there is that other type of conversation - *the awkward conversation.*

When you are in the midst of an embarrassing moment, you see yourself in a situation you wished you were not.

Hence, knowing what to do exactly in those moments will prepare you for the worst.

This book will help you on the ff:
- Importance of Speaking Tactfully
- What makes conversations awkward and how to avoid them?
- How to have perfect conversation with your partner?
- How to handle a conversation with your parents?
- Business and work conversations
- General Tips and Tricks to be a top speaker

Grab a copy of this book and start your journey into more assertive, confident, and tactful!

HOW TO SAY NO TO YOURSELF: CONQUERING INTERMITTENT FASTING 101- THE COMPLETE GUIDE FOR BEGINNERS & BUSY PEOPLE
(BONUS: NO-STRESS 30-DAY SIMPLE PLAN, MEAL PREPARATIONS, COOKBOOK AND MORE!)

Intermittent fasting is currently one of the most popular health and fitness trends in the world. It will teach you the unique process of following alternative fasting and feeding cycles.

This book contains proven steps and strategies on how to intermittently fast for weight loss and also examines the concept of clean nutrition.

By reading it, you will learn practical and proven arts and practices that, if followed religiously, will create a young, vibrant, exuberant, radiant and totally different being.

Do you have to lose weight? Are you trying to adapt to that new outfit for the summer? But you don't want to fall in love with those diets and lose weight with the quick tricks of the past, you need something that really stands the test of time. Much more than a diet, you need a change in lifestyle. This is exactly what the 30-day intermittent fasting challenge offers. Intermittent fasting can restart and restore the body, helping to put metabolic processes back on track. Fasting teaches your body to burn fat instead of complex carbohydrates.

With your body poised and ready to burn fat for fuel, stubborn fatty deposits like your belly, arms and legs will evaporate quickly! It may sound too good to be true, but only by regulating the body through a dedicated and consistent fasting regimen - this is truly possible! This book provides you with the knowledge, background, and recipes to successfully perform your intermittent fasting regime over the course of 30 days.

In this book you will get:

Why fast?

What is intermittent fasting?

Intermittent fasting and your hormones

Intermittent fasting and weight loss

Eat Healthily

The Keto diet

Autophagy and intermittent fasting

Pagan's diet

Intermittent fasting methods

Intermediate fasting benefits

Dangers of intermittent fasting

Intermittent fasting programs

And, in essence, everything you need to learn how to apply the practice of intermittent fasting to your life program to reap immense intrinsic benefits and thus become a healthier, happier, better and, yes, richer being.

SCAN ME

THE ADVENTURES OF SEPHAS
(SIMPLE BEDTIME STORIES FOR
KIDS: QUICK READ AND
ILLUSTRATIONS INCLUDED):

THE BOY WHO SPEAKS 100 LANGUAGES AND HELPS MANY PEOPLE ALL OVER THE WORLD

It is his 7th birthday; he got a gift. Little did he know what this gift can do for him ... Where will he go? What can he do? Can Sephas save the day?

Don't Forget to Claim your FREE ebook!

OTHER PROMOTED BOOKS

S. K. PILGRIM

I.K. BUTCHER

KENOSIS BOOKS: BE THE BEST YOU – SELF-IMPROVEMENT SERIES

SUBSCRIBE AND GET YOUR FREE eBOOK!

If you want to improve the quality of your attention and are willing to do other means to improve your focus and concentration, then this book will definitely help you in that. This book contains the ff:

1. Top Foods to increase your Focus and Concentration

2. Foods you can intake daily to improve your focus

3. Best Juices to Improve your focus

4. Healthy Habits and Eating Style to Improve Focus

..... and much more!

So take action, and scan the QR CODE and/or Subscribe to our **Kenosis Books - Be The Best You: Self-Improvement Series** *mailing list and be updated in our latest books and promotions!*

ABOUT THE AUTHOR

S.K. Pilgrim loves nature, travelling, food, and learning. He is a sport buff and loves running a lot. As a marathoner, he believes that keeping himself in good shape not only improves his running but also other aspects of his life. He loves reading books as well as writing them.

S.K. Pilgrim has a full-time job as senior leader in a multinational company. He is very passionate in coaching, training, and organizational development. He never gives up on any talent until they progress and improve to their potential!

Reach SK Pilgrim and our other authors in
kenosisbooks@gmail.com

Cheers!

BOOK BY THIS AUTHOR

GIGA-ENERGY: HIGH ENERGY FOOD
- TURN-AWAY FROM SWEETS AND
ENERGY DRINKS BONUS: LOW
CHOLESTEROL AND LOW SUGAR
ENERGY BOOSTERS

LOW ON ENERGY? HOW LONG CAN YOU SUSTAIN YOUR ENERGY?

Daily tasks and labor require a lot of energy but ending up on the vicious cycle of coffee, sweets, and high-energy drinks is detrimental to our health.

This book aims to share with you alternative sources of energy that will make you more energetic and last longer through more sustainable and healthy means.

- Instant Energy Boosters

- Long-term Energy Boosters
- Plant-Based Energy Boosters
- Juices and Smoothies Energy Boosters
- Daily Routines to Maintain Energy Levels
- Faster Metabolism and Weight Loss
- Energy-packed Breakfast
- and Much Much More!
- BONUS
  - Low-cholesterol Energy Boosters
  - Low-sugar Energy Boosters

Grab a copy of this book and let it lead you to GIGA-ENERGY lifestyle!

ABOUT THE AUTHOR

I.K. Butcher's passion for building a conducive workplace started when he was in university. He began studying people development and practiced it firsthand. He led teams not only into developing themselves but also directing them into purpose – most especially, the socially oriented one.

Butcher continued this passion when he moved to a consumer goods company after he achieved his university degree. For 12 years, he learned sales, capability building, and business development. He travelled to various places both domestically and internationally to hone his skills and share his lessons to new employees who have begun in their careers.

Butcher believes that one needs to learn multitudes of skills to really excel in an organization and that he is very much willing to share his experiences to help those who are really serious about such an endeavor.

Reach I. K. Butcher and our other authors in kenosisbooks@gmail.com!

BOOK BY THIS AUTHOR

MANAGING UPWARDS: THE
BEGINNER'S GUIDE IN MANAGING
YOUR BOSS (BONUS: THE SOFT SIDE:
HOW TO WIN YOUR BOSS BY
BUILDING A FRIENDLY
RELATIONSHIP)

Have you been struggling with your boss? Are you a start out with the management skills to workplace excellence? Do you simply fancy the topic and wish to be armed with the artillery for Managing your Boss?

Whatever the category you find yourself in, this book is poised to arm you with all the necessary strategies for starting and maintaining a healthy and synergistic relationship with your boss in such a way that your personal goals, that of your boss, and the overall objectives of your company are met.

Outlined in well thought of moves, you will be led through four exciting journeys of

✓   Self-identification, skill discovery and skill optimization

✓   Identifying the personal traits, strengths, weaknesses, and context of your boss

✓   Knowing the company, what it stands for, your role and that of your boss

✓   Bridging the gap where stark differences exist

The major chapters all end with action points, step to take to ensure proper use of the information you're provided with. For the young, for the experienced, for whoever seeks to stand out and succeed in the workplace, this is the book for you.

So, grab a copy now of this book and check out our exciting bonuses and free books that you can avail!

Don't Forget to Claim your FREE eBook!

Printed in Dunstable, United Kingdom